ON THE HUNT

BLACK BEAR HUNTING

BY ROXANNE TROUP

EPIC

EPIC, AN IMPRINT OF BELLWETHER MEDIA BY FLUTTERBEE

EPIC BOOKS are no ordinary books. They burst with intense action, high-speed heroics, and shadows of the unknown. Are you ready for an Epic adventure?

This edition first published in 2027 by Bellwether Media, Inc.

Bellwether Media is a division of FlutterBee Education Group.

For information regarding permission, write to Bellwether Media, Inc., Attention: Permissions Department, 3500 American Blvd W, Suite 150, Bloomington, MN 55431.

Library of Congress Cataloging-in-Publication Data

Names: Troup, Roxanne author
Title: Black bear hunting / by Roxanne Troup.
Description: Minneapolis, Minnesota : Bellwether Media, Inc, 2027. | Series: On the hunt | Includes bibliographical references and index. | Audience: Ages 8-12 | Audience: Grades 2-3 |
Summary: "Engaging images accompany information about black bear hunting. The combination of high-interest subject matter and light text is intended for students in grades 2 through 7"-- Provided by publisher.
Identifiers: LCCN 2026001566 (print) | LCCN 2026001567 (ebook) | ISBN 9798898800925 (library binding) | ISBN 9798898802165 (ebook)
Subjects: LCSH: Black bear hunting--Juvenile literature | Bear hunting--Juvenile literature | Hunting--Juvenile literature
Classification: LCC SK295 .T76 2027 (print) | LCC SK295 (ebook)
LC record available at https://lccn.loc.gov/2026001566
LC ebook record available at https://lccn.loc.gov/2026001567

Editor: Ashley Kuehl Designer: Jennifer Bowyer

Printed in the United States of America, North Mankato, MN.

TABLE OF CONTENTS

CHASING SHADOWS

The misty mountains are quiet. A hunter studies the hillside with **binoculars**.

A dark shape slips through the trees like a shadow. It is a black bear!

WHAT IS BEAR HUNTING?

Black bears have a large range. They live in forests and mountain areas throughout North America.

AMERICAN BLACK BEAR RANGE

Thirty-five states in the United States and all of Canada allow black bear hunting. People hunt bears in spring and fall.

In open areas, hunters **spot-and-stalk** bears. They look through binoculars. When they see a bear, they follow it.

TRIATHLETES

Like human athletes, black bears are strong and fast. They run, swim, and climb trees!

In other places, people hunt with **bait**. Sometimes dogs help hunters. Dogs chase bears up trees for hunters to find.

Bear hunting is a **tradition** for many hunters. People hunt with family. They enjoy the outdoors.

People eat bear meat. They use the bear **hide** for decoration.

FAVORITE HUNTING SPOT

TONGASS NATIONAL FOREST, ALASKA

- Largest population of black bears in North America
- Largest national forest in the U.S. covers nearly **26,500** square miles (68,790 square kilometers) of land

bear meat
bear hide

NEEDED GEAR

Hunters spend many days on a bear hunt. They bring food, water, and camping gear. Some hunters use mules to carry supplies. They keep **bear spray** and **ammo** in a backpack.

HUNTING GEAR

Bears have strong senses. They can hear and smell hunters. The hunter must shoot from far away.

Hunters use a **rangefinder** to find a bear. Hunters sneak closer. They set a rifle on a **bipod** to shoot.

After hunters clean their kill, they carry it on a pack frame.

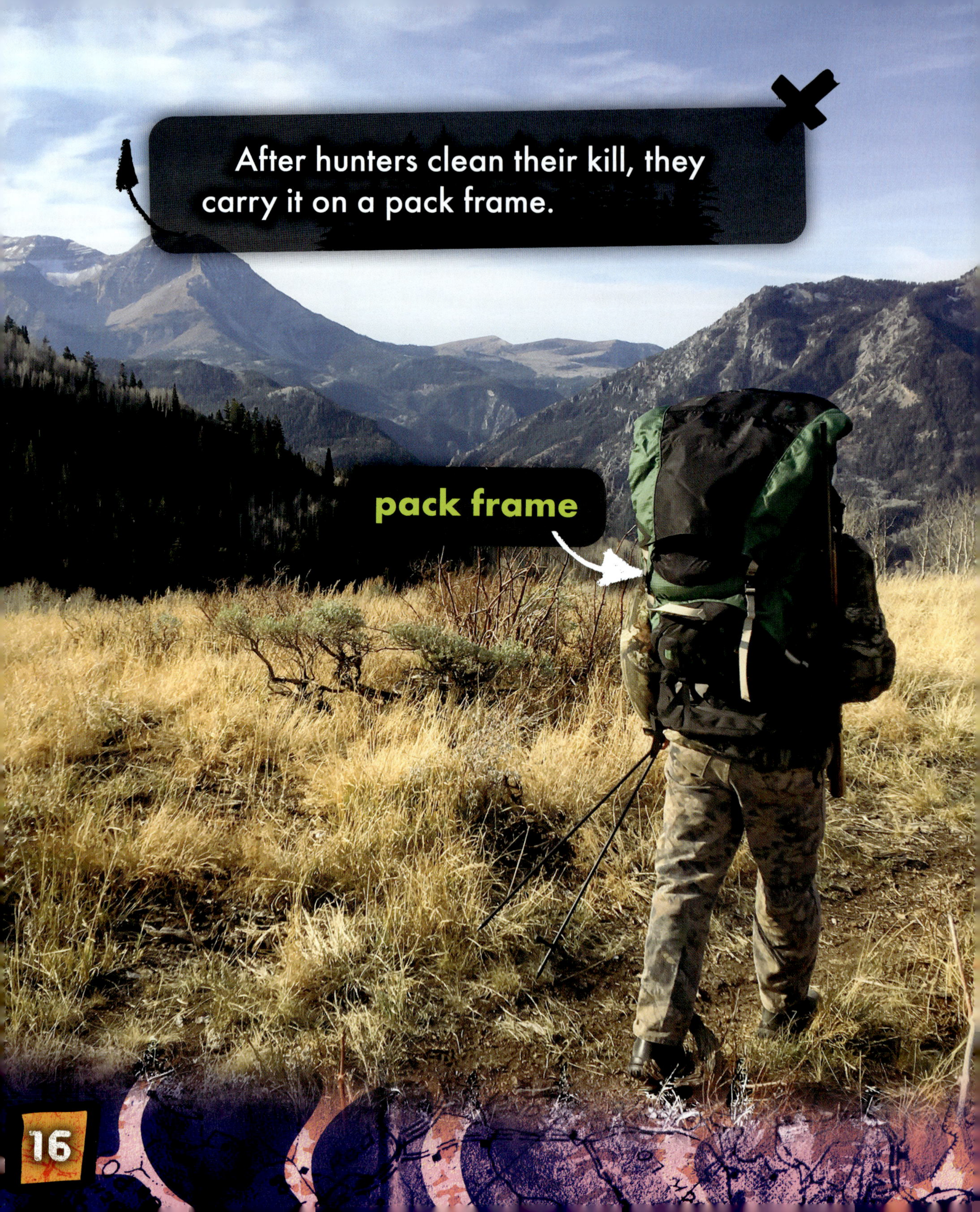

CURIOUS CRITTERS

Black bears are curious. They like to explore new smells and sounds. People often see bears searching cars, tents, and trash bins.

Bears are most active at sunrise and sunset. This is when they search for food. When it is dark, hunters wear headlamps.

SAFETY FIRST

Hunters must have a **license** to hunt bears. This limits the number of bears **harvested** each season.

COLORFUL COAT

Black bears' fur can be black, brown, blond, gray, or white. Their colors are different in different places.

In some areas, bear season overlaps other hunting seasons. Hunters wear **blaze orange** so other hunters can see them.

Bears have heavy bones and a thick hide. This makes them hard to kill. An injured bear may attack.

Hunters should practice before shooting a bear. Getting the bear on the first shot will keep people safe.

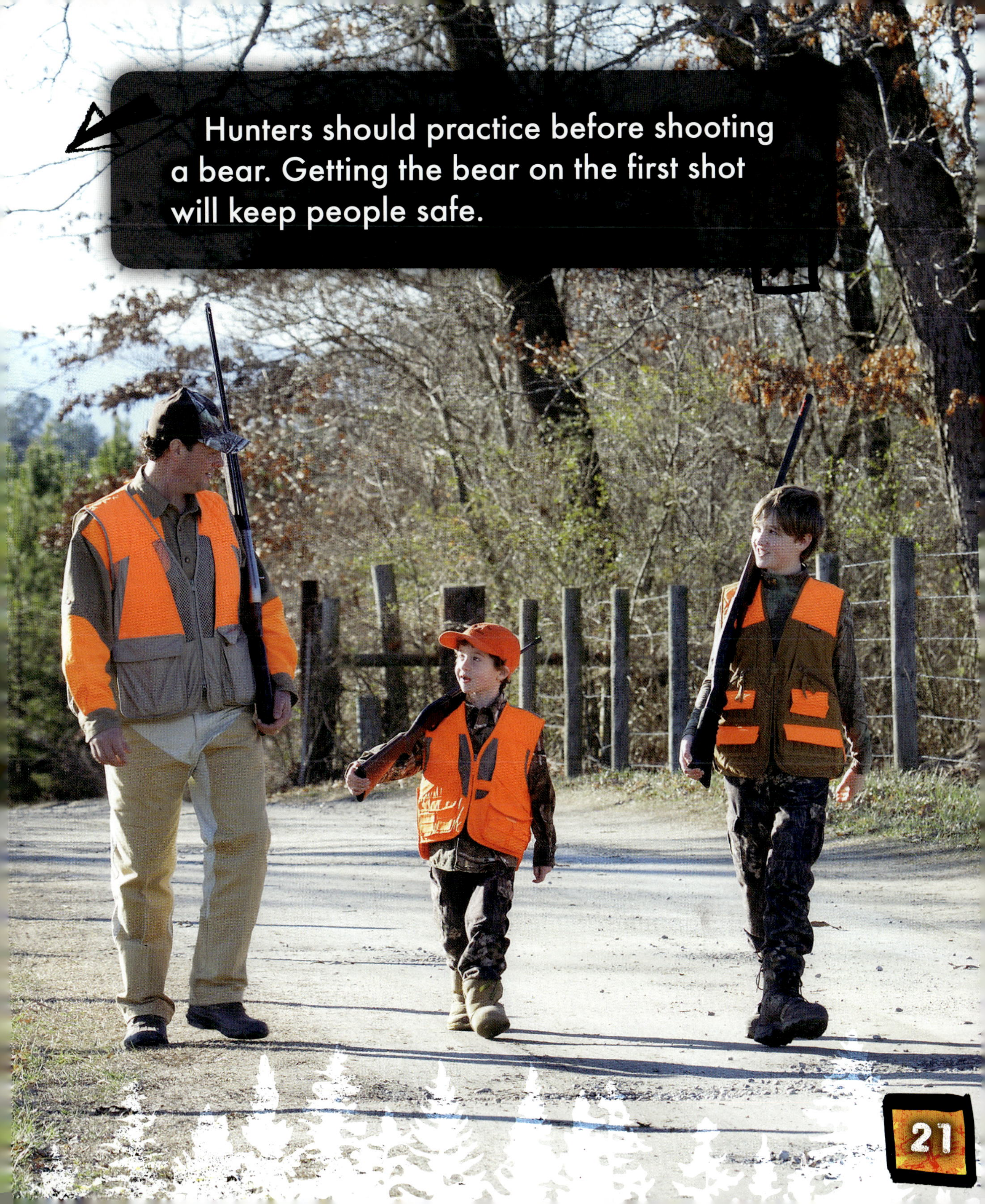

GLOSSARY

ammo—short for ammunition; ammo is often bullets.

bait—food left to attract an animal

bear spray—a substance that, if used on a bear, makes it hard for the bear to breathe and see, allowing a person to escape

binoculars—a device a person looks through that makes far-off objects appear closer

bipod—a stand with two legs that hunters rest a gun on

blaze orange—a bright orange color that hunters wear for safety

harvested—collected

hide—animal skin

license—a document that gives hunters legal permission to harvest a certain type of animal

rangefinder—a camera-like device that measures distance

spot-and-stalk—a hunting method in which hunters use binoculars to find prey and then follow that prey on foot

tradition—a custom, idea, or belief handed down from one generation to the next

TO LEARN MORE

AT THE LIBRARY

Brach, Kyle. *Big Game Hunting*. Minneapolis, Minn.: Lerner Publications, 2024.

Sommer, Nathan. *Black Bear vs. Mountain Lion*. Minneapolis, Minn.: Bellwether Media, 2025.

Troup, Roxanne. *Elk Hunting*. Minneapolis, Minn.: Bellwether Media, 2025.

ON THE WEB

FACTSURFER

Factsurfer.com gives you a safe, fun way to find more information.

1. Go to www.factsurfer.com.
2. Enter "black bear hunting" into the search box and click 🔍.
3. Select your book cover to see a list of related content.

INDEX

The images in this book are reproduced through the courtesy of: Lars Ove Jonsson, front cover, p. 1; Tracy, front cover, p. 1; ManoStudioArt, front cover, pp. 1, 3; Jim Cumming, front cover, p. 1; PRESSLAB, p. 4; mountinez, p. 5; CHRISTINA RADCLIFFE, p. 6; KenCanning, p. 7 (profile); Robert Nyholm, p. 7; Okyela, p. 8; ZUMA Press, Inc./ Alamy Stock Photo, p. 8 (bait); C_Gara, p. 9; visualspace, p. 11; Perry Mastrovito/ Alamy Stock Photo, p. 11 (hide); arnaudbouchard, p. 11 (meat); melissamn, p. 12; DieterMeyrl, p. 13 (rifle); Maxim Stukonozhenko/ Alamy Stock Photo, p. 13 (rangefinder); Erin Paul Donovan/ Alamy Stock Photo, p. 13 (spray); mmpixel91, p. 13 (binoculars); Cavan Images/ Alamy Stock Photo, p. 13 (headlamp); Paul Briden/ Alamy Stock Photo, p. 13 (tripod); Carol Hamilton, p. 14; Fertnig, p. 15; Kyle T Perry, p. 16; Benoit, p. 17; Spencer Platt/ Getty Images, p. 18; Don White, p. 19 (inset); BrandyTaylor, p. 19; Banyan Ranch Studios, p. 20; Wayne Hughes/ Alamy Stock Photo, p. 21; Nadezda Murmakova, p. 23.